TERRY McDONAGH

B
O
X
E
S

BLAUPAUSE
BOOKS

For
Seán and Matthew

Thanks are due to the many children
and colleagues I've worked with
for their inspiration.

Special thanks to Joanna.

I SBN 3-933498-12-0
© 2006 Blaupause-Books O. Hille
Sommerhuder Str. 6, D-22769 Hamburg, Germany
Cover illustration and Layout: Olaf Hille, Hamburg
mail@blaupause-books.com
www.blaupause-books.com

CONTENTS

AUTOMATIC BLINDS

At my old school, we got
new automatic blinds
that came down when the sun
was hot, and went up again
when it disappeared
behind a cloud. Our class
loved the blinds and prayed
for super sun and moody skies.

Some parents noticed their children
listening to the weather forecast
before school and wondered.

Weeks went by. We clapped and
chuckled at every little cloud
until one day our teacher ran away
to live high up a tree in the forest.

We were all really sad and sent her
flowers. A man with a ladder
came and took the blinds away.

The old curtains were put back up.
All together we wrote to our teacher
telling her of rain, rain, only rain.

She did return, and told stories
of the sun gods, eclipses and
dark winters in Scandinavia.

As before, she opened and closed
the curtains by hand, but nobody
would ever forget the automatic blinds.

HEAD LICE

I've had head lice
twice ...   scratch ... scratch.

Nearly went bananas, I did.
Worse than bad breath, it was!
Good mates defect to
enemy gangs, take the lice
with them and keep on

                                             scratching.

My things were put
in the freezer
to frostbite the life
out of the geezers ...   scratch.

I cried for my Teddy
in his cold, cold cot ...   scratch.

A teacher got lice four times.
The kids went wild and cheered.
The teacher went home ...   scratch.

They get into hair
and into clothes
and onto pillows
and onto car seats
and onto toys
and onto teddies
and onto friends.

They get around ...   scratch.

One kid took
a photo of a louse
and enlarged it.
It looked like a mouse.
A small girl fainted.
Oh, my God!   Scratch!

Some say super lice
that can't be killed
are on the way.
Don't let this happen,
please …   scratch.

My friend said
her whole class
had head lice
at her last school
and they scratched

                                        and scratched

                    dehctarcs dna.

scratch
scratch

scratch   scratch

scratch   **scratch**   *scratch*
scratch

9

DREAM-TREE-HOUSE

I'm older now and our tree
is gone but I still long for
the dream-tree-house
my grandfather built for us
before frantic rock and
savage metal drove
our ghosts away. I think
we were happy till then.

When the factory came
old trees fell
        like stars
in winter,
        high-rise flats
dropped
      into the valley
and the river gave way
to a car park.
Everything died, except
for swearing and cement.

We got our fish from
fish farms – frozen,
meat from cages – frozen,
milk from the fridge,
potato puree and cheese
from overseas.

Now that the factory is closed,
we are left high up here
among loose power lines
and rattling windows.

Some curious birds and animals
have come back to try again
but we are too weak to cheer them on.

THE FIRE ALARM

Our class is quiet today
because Miss Cardigan
is telling us about our
fire-alarm system.

While she is droning on about
escape-route doors and extinguishers,
little Thomas is dreaming of pushing
the red fire-alarm button.
It would be so much
fun!

In his mind, he can see
happy kids racing in all
directions:
without schoolbags,
through blazing classrooms,
in football gear,
in the rain,
in snow,
in sunshine,
in springtime,
in autumn,
in winter,
at nine o clock,
at two,
at twelve,
day and night,
during maths,

when Miss C. is angry
– never in the holidays
or at weekends.

He sees himself
pushing the button
time and time again,
one false alarm
after another,
minute by minute,
hour by hour,
day after day,
week in week out,
year after year,
forever and ever,
till the end of time.

THE JAIL BIRD

The jail bird on our road
doesn't even look like a bird
but he's been to jail
for bank robbery,
I overheard a neighbour say.

I peeped over the hedge
when he was in his garden
and was hugely disappointed
to see him pruning apple trees
and trimming hedges.

I'd hoped he'd be cleaning his gun,
or making masks at the back door.
I wanted to see him stacking
bank notes or hiding jewels
under a rose bush. But no!
all he did was water the flowers
and mow the lawn.

One afternoon, I saw him leave
the house.
                    Trembling,
I shadowed him
all the way to the bank.
In he went.
I called the police
and hid at the corner.

There was noise
and chaos everywhere.
It was brilliant!

At breakfast Mum said
I'd been calling out 999
in my sleep.
'Are you feeling...?'
'Fine, Mum. I'm fine.'

The jail bird was planting daisies
as I passed
on my way to school.

I wonder what he keeps
in his tool shed.

THE LIAR

There's this new guy
in our class
who just can't tell the truth.
He makes me so angry.

He's seen everything.
He's done everything.
He's richer than everyone.
He's better at sport than us.
He's been everywhere.

His clothes cost the earth.
He stays out late.
He's got his own telly.
He's a year older and
he's good-looking, of course!

My friend says it's all true.
She's seen his house
and his father's car.

But I don't believe her
because she likes him
and I can't stand him!

He's so full of himself.
A liar, for sure.

POTHOLES AND PUDDLES

It rained last night and
this morning the potholes
on our road were full.
I'd be late for school
but didn't care.

When I looked into one,
I could see a deep kingdom
where fish were friends
and fishermen hooked each other
high above on the raging pier.

There were detective sharks
on the lookout for teachers' pets
and dancing dolphins
biting into swot backsides.

In another pothole, there were
fat heaps full of fizz and cake
at dozens of birthday parties.

I'll be eight tomorrow and
my mother won't be home.
I'd like to play with my friend
but he's away visiting his dad
in prison. I wish my granny
didn't smoke all the time.

I've still got two puddles
to go.

RULES

Stop talking!
Listen to me!
Be quiet!
Be on time!
Sit down!
Learn it by heart!
Stand up!
Ask your mother!
Dress properly!
Sit up straight!
Read good books!
Don't watch TV!
Do your homework!
Don't be late!
Wipe your feet!
Close the door!
Speak properly!
Repeat after me!
Watch your tenses!
Behave yourself!
Don't be cheeky!
Start again!

Time for bed.
Time to get up.
Time for school.
Time for home.
Time for homework.
Time for bed.

Time for TV?
Time for friends?
Time for football?
Time for internet?
Time for hanging out?
Time for cinema?

Teachers and parents
just don't know
the score.
They never did
and never will.

When I grow up
I'll live with
my kids among
the stars – without
school or rules
or school rules.

BOXES

One day, our teacher
put boxes of different colours
in a row and asked us
to choose one
and tell the class
what we thought
was in it.
We were to use our imagination.
It was fun.

I said there was a sleepy horse
in the smallest yellow box.
She asked me if the horse
was a big horse and I said,
'Yes, he's a giant horse.'
My friends laughed.
I said it again for effect.
'He's a big, giant lazy horse,
big as a house in the sky!'

They laughed even louder.
I wanted to say more
but teacher screamed,
'That's enough!'

One of the girls had a red box
full of soldiers and hungry children
in a desert. She said she would put
food and roses in her box each day.

The new quiet boy said
his blue box was empty.
No one believed him.
Someone asked what he'd like
to have in his box
and he replied, he'd like
to have his dad at home in it

My friend said, there was
a dancing pencil in her
black box and
when the lid came off
the pencil would write on the wind.

I HOPE SO

Sometimes, when my class
is quiet and working,
I sit wondering what they
will be doing in twenty years.

Some will have children
of their own, a few will
be rich and like money.

One of them might be famous
and wallow in bright lights and
the sound of clapping.

They look so busy, sitting
thinking of answers to problems
in books. Are some of them
dreaming of coloured stars,
fairy pebbles on a faraway shore
or life behind the moon?

Will they make the world
a better place for children?
Will they always cry when
a pet dies or a special friend
has to leave them?

Do they sometimes think
the book is daft, or that I am
a little silly. I hope so.
I am happy here with my
class. I wonder if one of them
will, one day, sit watching
their class? I hope so.

THE HUNT

I will always remember
being eleven and petrified
at the sight of a grown man
– in full flight –
being swallowed up
by hedges and gorse bushes,
with a fat policeman and
a handful of neighbours, armed
with pitchforks and sticks,
in hot pursuit.
Dogs barked in the distance.

They gave up the chase
when he took a fence
in his stride.
I was relieved to see him
top the hill
and disappear forever
into my imagination.

MY FRIEND JIM

My friend, Jim, rides
to school on his pony.
He doesn't use a saddle.
While other kids are
getting out of cars, he
is tethering Starkey
to a tree by the stream.

Jim hasn't been with us long
and he won't be staying.
He's a traveller from all over.

He dreams he's going to build
a big-top with strings to the stars
and he'll comb galaxies
for a lightning steed
more elegant than any thoroughbred
in the land of Ireland.

My dad doesn't want Jim
coming round our way
                   – travellers steal,
he says.
                   Jim's my friend.

One day he gave me
a piece of shiny glass
from his mother
                   to bring me luck.
Another time he gave me
stones in different colours.

I keep them out of sight
under my mattress and
only take them out when
the moon fills my bedroom.
They glow like singing
in the copper corner.

I feel strong and grateful
to my friend, Jim.

One day, we'll share
the roads of this country.
I just know we will.

PLAYING WITH FIRE

Two boys lit a piece of paper
in the toilet. Someone saw
smoke. There was chaos.

Their teachers couldn't understand it.
'I don't understand. Why?'

Their parents couldn't understand it.
'We don't understand. Why?'

The principal couldn't understand it.
'It won't ever happen again at our school.'

Again and again,
they were asked,
why?
why?
why?
why?
why?
why?
why?
why?
why?
why?
why?
why?
why?
why?
why?

why?
why?
why?
why?
why?
Twenty times.

One boy said, he didn't know
and the other boy said
he liked playing with fire.

ALEXANDER

All the lads in our class
liked Alex. The girls
didn't. He wasn't cool.
When he missed
the ball, he laughed
and the boys did.
The girls didn't.
The teacher was a girl
teacher. When his
pen
         fell,
the boys sniggered.
The girls didn't.
When he said
he loved a frog, the boys
exploded –
         the girls didn't:
– *he's stupid!*

When he bent
         down
for
  his
         pen,
the teacher fell over
his
         bottom
and landed on
her
         head.

She went to hospital.
The boys giggled.
The girls didn't. Alex
didn't. Alex fell on
the ball. He didn't
laugh. The boys
didn't. The girls did.

He was alone with the ball
and didn't know how to play.

The teacher returned.
She didn't smile. Alex
didn't. The boys
didn't. The girls
didn't. Alex cried a lot
at home.
The fourth class
didn't laugh much for a while.

PLAYING HORSEY

Standing by a school wall
I watched a group of children
playing horsey
in a corner of the playground
with the autumn wind
tossing dust and dead leaves
in upon them.

They didn't seem
to notice. They just
kept on trading
and grooming
with nothing, but
a piece of cord
and wild imagination
to warm them.

Straining up high
in their stirrups,
they could see
the whole world.

THE PRIMARY PUPPET

While bombs were falling
on Asian soil, the puppet class
was called upon
to down tools and listen
to the President's master plan
in case of a bomb threat:

'We will run to an open field.
You will be safe in that field.'

'It is a model battlefield,'
he assured them.
'There are flags for everyone'
– he had his directives from
on high, he said.

One bemused girl asked
if they could wear masks
as a form of protection.
The President said,
'Yes! A novel idea'

There could be blackened faces
like brave soldiers,
and gas masks
in case of fallout.

They all giggled.
He didn't.

'War is a serious business.
It will always be with us.'

A senior student suggested
they read poetry and sang
in the open field – and
it might rain. The President
clicked his heels and said
there would be no talking,
noise or absurdities in public
– in particular
on fields of battle and,
as a senior student,
                          she should know
that poetry and singing
belonged to choirs and classrooms.

'If you want to be silly later in life,
you can join a theatre company.'

They were now at school
learning the hard facts.
When the war was over,
visual arts students would
be working on a monument
to an unknown soldier, and
young poets could write laments
to their dead heroes.

One student took a puppet
out of his pocket
and held it up for all to see.

'And what is that, young man?'
'It's a puppet, Sir.'
'It looks like a soldier.'
'It is a soldier, Sir.'

The President scratched
his head. He was happy to say
there would be an information screen
with honours lists
and military updates
along the hedgerows.

A small boy made his way
to the front, raised his hand
and politely asked
where the field was.

The President looked confused
but reassured the boy
it was on its way, and
it would do us proud.

All but one of the class
took out their puppets.

WHY CAN'T WE HAVE OUR OWN GODS?

My friend was born Christian.
I was born Jew.
We go to the same school,
live in the same street,
like wearing the same clothes,
like eating the same food,
love swimming,
love playing volleyball,
don't like doing homework,
don't like getting up.

I go to the synagogue
on Saturday.
She goes to church
on Sunday.

My mother tells me,
we are the Chosen People.

My friend's mother tells her,
their God is their Saviour.

I told my mother and
she told her mother
we had seen gods laughing,
singing and dancing together
in a circle of moonlight.

They both said, we
couldn't have: 'You are
too young to understand
but, one day, you will.'

But we do understand!

We talk to our gods
who dance with us
in the moonlight.

NEW FLARES

Last week, I bought
a pair of trousers
– flares!
and home I went
full of joy, only
to hear from my mother
her flares used to be
almost identical

                    – better even!
Hers were bellbottoms.

She knows as well
as I do that flares
are new
and have never been
worn before.

'I'm different,'
I told her.

She laughed, but
I know she was
jealous
and only wanted
to upset me
so I stormed off
to my room
and banged the door.

'Who does she think
she is?'

I was upset,
mad,
angry,
raging,
furious.

Typical parents,
adults,
grown ups

to suggest that flares
were worn
in their time.
They're too old
to remember.

I will never tell lies
to my children.
It isn't fair.

Okay, they might
have had flares
but never like ours.
I told her that
at tea. I didn't care
how she felt.

My best friend
has the same problem
with her mother.

Flares are just
one example.

IF I CAN, I WILL

Tom is the new class representative.

Before the elections, Tom promised:
'If I win, there will be free drinks
for everyone at Christmas.'

One girl pledged: 'If I win,
we will have less homework.'

And a boy gave his word: 'If I win,
we will have more class trips.'

The teacher counted the votes
and Tom won by a single vote.

The new quiet girl cried
because she got no votes.

At home, Tom's father asked
about his first meeting with
all the other class representatives.
Tom said, the others were
bigger and older and
it was boring – he didn't
understand them, anyway.
'But the voting was fun, Dad!'

'You must try to keep
your promise to the class, Tom.'

'If I can, I will, Dad.'

'If you can't get cola for everybody
what will you do, Tom?'

'When is Christmas, Dad?'

His dad smiled.

'If I can, I'll help, Tom.'

'Thanks, Dad.'

Tom likes his dad.

TEACHERS' DRESS

We girls in the fourth class think
our teachers dress badly,
look weird
                    – like parents.
We don't want to mention names
but our principal doesn't polish
her shoes, and Miss Smart,
 the tall teacher, wears funny jeans
and sandals with grey socks.
A friend's mother saw her coming
out of a pub, singing and carrying
a goose she had won playing poker.

One gentle, pale lady paints her nails,
wears too much lipstick
and likes discos and muesli.
She looks cool, a bit impractical
like a parrot or somebody special.

Our favourite teacher is a man.
He wears yellow ties and looks
tired in the mornings –
                    he's not married.

The pale lady
and the man with ties
look nice together.
We see them talking
in the car park – giggling
after school, but
they drive home
in separate cars.

That's sad, we think.

A CLASS-PROJECT ON
THE BEATLES

'Let's do a project on The Beatles, class?' Blank
faces. A small voice said:
'They are very old. Granddad remembers their
music. He wore their shoes.'
'Shoes?'
'Yeh, pointy ones. One Beatle was murdered.'
'Murdered!'
'In America. John something.'
'My dad will know.'
'He's too young.'
The teacher turned pale.

(This fifty word Mini-Saga was short-listed for *The Daily Telegraph* prize.)

MICHAEL

Michael used to be a pest,
a nuisance in class.

'He's a bright boy,
but...'
    the teacher
wrote to his parents.

'He's a good boy
but...'
    the principal
wrote to his parents.

He was sent home,
grounded,
given extra work,
no pocket money,
his swimming even stopped.

His parents were called in
to discuss Michael.
They came on separate days
to do their best for their son:

'He's a good boy, really.'
'He isn't a bad boy.'

Michael joined Young Writers
at school and put his wish
into four lines:

'I wish my mum and dad
and my sister and me
could all be together in a house
by the sea. That's my wish.'

When he had read it
to the group,
he seemed happier.

The teacher made two copies
and sent them to his parents' homes.

NOTHING'S FAIR

What's all this about fairness?
Nothing's fair when
you're a kid. Parents
can fight all they want to
and it's okay –
they can even divorce.
When kids have fights,
it's big stuff:
no pocket money, lines
TV withdrawal threats.

Just last week, I tried
to fly my new UFO
from our upstairs window
and just because it landed
on Mrs Murphy's cat, I'm
out of favour –
                    in the doghouse.

Oh, I can go to school,
all right – even to
my daft piano lessons
but I can't repair my UFO.
I'm a threat to the neighbourhood.

When Dad crashed the car,
Mum put her arms round him.
He was in shock, poor man.
I'm in a permanent state of shock
and I get my freedom chopped.

Dad's driving again.
Mum's more loving than ever
to him
                          – to me she's horrible,
just because my invention
killed Murphy's black cat.

Nothing's fair when you're a kid.
I'll create chaos when I'm older.
I'll get my own back. I will!

THE ANARCHIST

I am a third class anarchist.
That's what Miss Frost said.
I tried to tell my mum
that our teacher got angry
just because I stood up
and went for a walk
during silent reading.
I had finished my work and
only wanted to look out at
the older boys playing football.
I like football.
'You must behave in class,
no matter what.'
'but I do, Mum.'

Once, I saw a pink pigeon
daydreaming on the wires
and another time, I saw
a flying cow on the page.
The girls said I was stupid
– that cows didn't fly.
Miss Frost gave me a cold look
and told me to sit down
and stop disturbing.

I don't tell my mother everything.

I can be very happy
just looking out the window,
watching too much telly
or playing football with

my new shoes in mud.
I hate homework.

I saw Mum smile when I told her
I liked doing things properly
most of the time, but when
spiders crept out of corners,
or snowflakes blew into drifts,
I forgot myself and went for a look.

'What's an anarchist, Mum?'

TONE-DEAF-PETER

Peter goes to school
at the usual time
on Tuesdays –
                          late,
to miss singing.
He hates standing
in a straight row
with his mouth
opening and closing
like a baby crow
in a hungry nest.

Peter likes singing,
and when he thinks
nobody's listening,
he sings in his head
like a rock-star in bed.

He's sung to his cat,
even to a thrush
in a summer bush.

What he doesn't like
is having to be quiet
standing in a row
with his mouth opening
and closing
while others are singing.

Christmas is the worst.

BEST FRIENDS

I have a best friend.
We do everything together.
She comes to my house:
to my mum,
to my dad,
to my colours,
to my dog,
to my baby brother,
to my room,
to my dreams,
to my friends,
to my books,
to my swimming,
to my music,
to my stories,
to my tears,
to my secrets,
and she, sometimes,
stays over at weekends.

Next year, she is leaving
for another country.
I'll be sad, but I know
we'll be best friends
forever. Mum says so.

JIMMY AND JOE

Jimmy, the monkey, had been
on Joe's shoulder for an age.
They were both old. One day,
Jimmy fell off after lunch
and that was that.
Try as they might there was
no way back up. He would
have to go to the nursing home
for ageing monkeys at the zoo.
Joe would take him there
in his rickety old banger.

The old monkey wasn't happy.
He huffed. He puffed.
He brooded in his bedroom.
They both cried big tears.
Joe promised to visit.

Next day, dressed in their best
and hand-in-hand
they hobbled to the car.
It wouldn't start.

Just then, a lonely young man
– without monkey experience –
chanced to pass.
Their red eyes moved him to stack
his right shoulder to the earlobe
with monkey nuts and bananas.

He said his name was Joe Young,
a blacksmith, used to carrying loads.

Jimmy knew which side
his bread was buttered on
when he hinted Joe Young
might move in with them.

One day, after Jimmy
had grown used to his new perch
and the sun was high
in the spring sky, the trio
set off to visit the zoo in Dublin.

They did the rounds of cages.
Jimmy chatted with old friends
about the perils of the forests,
cold life in captivity and
the importance of love in your life.
They all agreed in a flurry of screeches
and Jimmy thanked his Joes with
kind pats on their bald spots.

With the young man at the wheel,
the old man and Jimmy slept,
dreamed and snored softly
all the way home.
They woke in time to see
their little cottage smile in
a splash of moonlight.

BACK-SEAT KIDS

The back seats in our classroom
are scratched, written on
and the legs are loose.

Front seats can never be
back seats
and back seats can never be
front seats –
                        they just can't.

Back-seat kids are kept in
more often. They wear
baseball caps sideways,
try to be cool and stick
chewing gum under seats.

They spend a lot of time
outside Mr Principal's door
waiting to be called in
for throwing a schoolbag
over the fence,
a small child's lunch
down the toilet, or
spilling paint in the art room.

But:
school back seats,
cinema back seats,
or bus back seats
– all back seats
fill up first

because back seats
are back seats
and the action is
at the back
in the back seats
yeh!
We are the back-seat
boys,
back-seat people
in back seats.
Back seats are
cool!
The best seats
are back seats
for back-seat kids
and kids from the
back seats. Yeh!

AMONG THE DEAD

The Cill Aodain graveyard gate
is always open. Nobody tries
to get in or out. Monks used
to sleep in the beehive hut,
and the remains of a church
and a few gravestones
are still standing.
                    I have the bones
of a poem in my pocket
and I can't help wondering
if my great relative in the corner
would turn in his grave
if I took it out and began
reading aloud in full moonlight.

SHIRLEY TEMPLE CURLS

Mum under the dryer, drinking coffee
with eight-year-old Sharon
on the next chair
being curled down to the wishbone
by a pair of hard-hearted hairdressers
on the morning of big sister's wedding.

This dragging, tugging, curling,
heating and clipping was worse
than being punched, or
having your hair pulled
by silly boys on the playground.

'The Shirley Temple look,'
one hairdresser reassures her.

'Is this person still alive?'
'Alive? Why do you ask?'

Sharon didn't answer, but threw
a sidelong glare at her mother, then
a questioning look in the mirror at
the row of adults waiting for hairdos.

She wondered about them and
she tried to picture a poor little girl
by the name of Shirley Temple.

A BOY'S LIFE ON EARTH

The hardest journey on earth
is that endless trip
down the supermarket aisle
between shelves of toys
with your mother dragging you
by the hand and you screaming
hardly an inch from a talking teddy
or a second from a button
that could set a galaxy on fire.

And you tell me life is fun, Mum!

You kick, throw yourself down,
promise not to buy, just look,
maybe hold for a second,

while she entertains herself with paint
for the railings, offers on toothpaste,
tedious trolleys, boring bread
and tins of kitty for the cat family

– no milkshakes, nothing tasty
from the lower shelves,
only up and down the healthy lane
among chattering mothers,
big sisters with lads, or dads
with hairy noses and bald patches.

Worst of all is when friends of the family
pick you up and half strangle you
poking overfed faces into yours:
'And how's our cute little man, today?'

And you tell me life is fun, Mum!

I'll scratch the baby
if this goes on much longer.

HAVIN THE CRAIC

After school by the bike shed,
Joe, the lads and me
were chewin the fat,
havin the *craic* about fightin
an laughin about sisters
an what we hate for breakfast,
an all that, when Joe's older sister
burst out gigglin on the other side
of the wall. She'd been listenin.
Joe went red, cos he'd been sayin
he never touched porridge
– only cornflakes, an his sister
tried to be bossy, an on the side
of the parents, an all that.

Her mates must have been with her
as well, cos we could hear them
laughin about us an singin, na,na,
nana, na, way down the road.
We said nothin, cos Joe was bigger
than us, an he was always chewin.

POETRY DOESN'T PAY

When a boy of eleven or twelve
asked me if I'd give up poetry
for a million in cash,
I had to think long and hard

about my next line.

BIOGRAPHY AND PUBLICATIONS:

Terry McDonagh, poet, dramatist and teacher, has lived in Hamburg for more than twenty years. He has had residencies in many countries in Europe, Asia and Australia. He now lives between Hamburg and Ireland. In addition to his books, his work has appeared in literary journals and anthologies, worldwide. *Boxes* is his first collection of poetry for young people.

Publications:

Poetry:
1 *The Road Out* – Olaf Hille Verlag, Hamburg – 1993.
2 *A World Without Stone* – Blaupause Books, Hamburg - 1998.
2 *A Song for Joanna* – Blaupause Books, Hamburg – 2002.
3 Included in: *Something beginning with P* – (anthology of Children's poetry) O'Brien Press, Dublin – 2004.

Poetry in translation:
4 *Kiltimagh* – (into German) Blaupause, Hamburg. Translation by Mirko Bonné. (Grant-aided by Ireland Literature Exchange – 2001).
5 *Tiada Tempat di Rawa* – (into Indonesian) Indonesia Tera, Magelang, Indonesia. Translated by Sapardi Djoko Damono and Dami N. Toda. (Grant-aided by Ireland Literature Exchange – 2004).

Prose:
6 *Elbe Letters go West / Briefe von der Elbe* – Blaupause Books, Hamburg – 1999.
7 *One summer in Ireland* – (A short novel for young people) Ernst Klett Verlag, Stuttgart – 2002.
8 Included in: *Weihnachtsgeschichten am Kamin* – Rowohlt Verlag, Reinbek. (a Christmas story: translation from English by Rainer Kuehn) – every Christmas since 1997.

Drama:
9 *I Wanted to Bring You Flowers/Ich kann das alles erklären* – Fischer Verlag, Aachen – 1991.

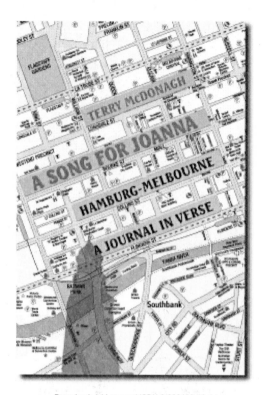

Paperback / 44 pages / ISBN 3-933498-10-4

This new collection finds Terry McDonagh in a foreign
country again – this time a visitor to a place with familiar
tongue – Australia. The beauty of this journal in verse is
that it arrives assured and mature from the opening line,
and with that same meditative voice we expect from a poet
of McDonagh's quality.

Joachim Matschoss, originally from Hamburg,
poet and dramatist in Melbourne